Pennine Walls

by

Arthur Raistrick

Dalesman Books
1988

The Dalesman Publishing Company Ltd.,
Clapham, via Lancaster, LA2 8EB.

First published 1946

Tenth impression (in new format) 1988

ISBN: 0 85206 929 4

Printed by Fretwell & Cox Ltd.,
Goulbourne Street, Keighley, West Yorkshire BD21 1PZ

Contents

1   Origin of the Walls 5

2   Building the Walls 13

3   Builders of the Walls 22

    For Further Study 31

*Line drawings, map and photographs by
Dr. Raistrick.*

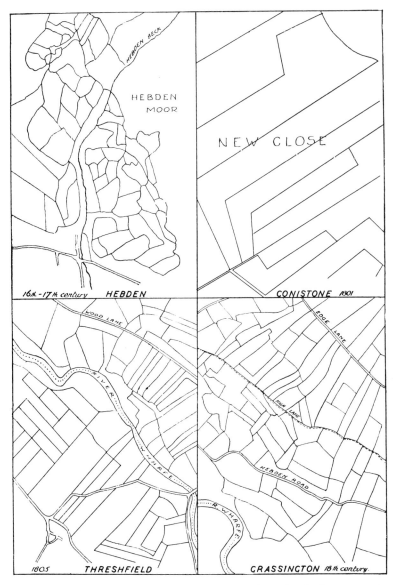

Field wall patterns in four adjacent townships. These show clearly the great variety in pattern and the steady development to straight ruled walling under the Enclosure Commissioners, seen in the Conistone New Close walls and the Threshfield walls south of the river. All are to the same scale.

4

1.   Origin of the Walls

MANY visitors to the Dales Country are at once attracted and puzzled by the miles and miles of stone walls that cover the valleys in a maze, and climb up the fell sides, disappearing in the distance over the highest summits. The true-born North Country man would feel that something vital was taken from the landscape if the intricate pattern of grey or brownish black walls, the deep velvety lines of shadows that they cast, and the brilliance of their sunlit tops were missing. The lovely, rounded contours of the Cheviots, the gaunt mountains of much of Scotland, seem at first sight strangely familiar, and yet strangely different to the visitor from the Dales; the fells and the moorland tops, the streams and gorges, are all familiar, but the absence or rarity of walls dividing up the wide expanse of country rob the views of a familiar pattern and texture which seem a natural part of the Pennine slopes.

When was this pattern of walls superimposed on our countryside? Who built the walls, why and how? These are frequent questions that one hears not only from occasional visitors, but from Dales born and bred people as well. The answer to these simple questions will need to be lengthy, the vast mileage of the walls, the hundreds, even thousands of square miles of country enclosed by them, alone make them worthy of a considered answer. First let us regard them as a pattern overlaid on the countryside. The pattern has appeared very differently to different people, and these differences have significance. Here are three fairly recent descriptions of walls in the Dales. 'The stone walls run up the hills in lines and squares like an old geometrical design whose meaning has long been lost' (Pontefract). 'You will see the land partitioned by stone walls into curiously irregular conformations, as unsymmetrical and grotesque as if they had been planned by some freakish surveyor in a fit of madness' (Riley). 'At first the walls took a bee-line track up the hillside, but when they reached the higher ground, where scars of rock and patches of reedy swamp lay in their path, their progress became serpentine' (Moorman). These three descriptions are made by people of keen observation, and in spite of their apparent contradictions they are essentially true and correct. The irregular crooked walls that follow a grotesque pattern are to be seen near any village or hamlet, and immediately around many outlying farmsteads. A maze of small enclosures, crofts and tiny fields, with scarcely a straight wall among them, surrounds the villages. Outside this maze lies the geometric, roughly rectangular pattern of the valley bottom and lower fell slopes, with fields from a few acres to twenty or more acres in extent, mainly walled with straight sections of walling, but curiously intermixed, small fields cut out of the sides or even the centre of larger fields, long and narrow fields, and short and square fields, with here and there one that is triangular or L-shaped. Here is the widespread pattern that we see from any of the valley roads anywhere in the Dales. On the higher ground, we all know the straight bee-line walls that go sometimes for miles without a deviation from their line except for an occasional serious obstruction that is by-passed. These walls are fewer and their pattern much broader than the others; they run from the top of the steeper valley side across the moors to the distant watershed, parcelling the moors into long strips with only occasional cross walls.

There are minor variations on these three themes but in the main these represent the three types and periods of walling dominant in the Dales and belong, very approximately, to the 16th, late 18th and early 19th centuries respectively. In their own way, each pattern of walling is a monument to a social and political revolution of first magnitude, as well as to the patience and skill of their builders. Before we discuss the craft of walling and the people who made the walls, let us look at the changes in social and economic structure which inspired the building of the walls.

In the Pennine valleys, the farming in general practice throughout the Middle Ages was a legacy and offspring of the system brought by the Anglo–Danish settler of the 7th and 10th centuries. In the upper Dales, the Norse shepherd stock of the 10th and 11th centuries added their quota to the customary farming and utilised land high up on the fellsides that the Anglo–Danes were unable or unwilling to cultivate. In all the area the common-field system was in vogue, with something of a threefold zoning of the land round each settlement. Along the rich valley bottom, near the rivers and on the flats so liable to winter floods, the Angles found ideal ground for their familiar 'water-meadows'; the 'leys' and 'ings' which were permanent meadow, in which every householder of the village had his apportioned or balloted share each year, undivided and unfenced from the rest, but sometimes marked by boundary stones at the end of the different strips, marked with a simple device of a cross, a triangle, or other mark. Such boundary stones of the meadow portions still remain in a few places; particularly they are to be seen on the ings between Cross Hills and Steeton. The whole meadowland was bounded by ditch and fence, the bank set with thorn or blackthorn trees, but with no sub-dividing fences. On drier ground there were the two or three common fields of the community, like the meadows bounded by ditch and bank but not sub-divided. Outside these was the common pasture and waste, extending up the hills and across the moors to the edge of the next settlement.

From the 12th century onward, as population increased and the numbers of sheep and cattle on the commons grew larger, disputes and accusations of trespass of sheep and stock from the waste of one village on to that of the next became common. A typical dispute is that in 1279 between the tenants of Fountains Abbey on the Malham moors, and the tenants of Salley Abbey, on the Stainforth and Langcliffe moors, each accusing the other of allowing their stock to wander and feed on the other's ground. The grangers of the two abbeys at Kilnsey and Stainforth Granges were ordered to mark the disputed boundaries with great stones, and mark the stones with great crosses, so that the extent of the pasture might be clear. Following many such disputes, the boundaries of the wastes between villages and townships were gradually marked out, either by agreement upon some natural feature, a beck or ridge, or by boundary crosses, or by a ditch and bank.

There is occasional evidence in the monastic cartularies of the early walling of fields and enclosures. Among the same group of deeds as those just quoted is the record of another dispute, this time between Fountains and Bolton, in which Bolton took measures to prevent the extension of walled enclosures on Cawdon in Malham '. . . also that the walls raised by the Abbott and Convent in Caluedon shall remain in that state in which they were at Easter 1257 . . .' Other grants in Malham indicate that the monks had already begun to wall with stone in several places, and there are several disputes over taking the stone from the common fields. At Salley Abbey grants of land in Salley included stone to build walls '. . . also they may enclose 2 acres with other three acres with a fosse and stone wall, the stone to be taken on his land.' It is clear from the documents for these and many other properties that the monks were already, in the 13th century, favouring the enclosure of small fields by stone walls which would prevent the trespass of animals on to their land, but that this cut right across the common practice and customs of the time.

In the 16th century, as the wool trade flourished and better breeds of sheep were introduced, great attention was given to their grazing and to the improvement of pastures, and parts of the outlying moors and wastes were then fenced in for the first time, to form more restricted pasture easier of control. From deeds of the period it is clear that many of these fences were stone walls, made partly for durability, and partly to clear the land of loose stones. Many indentures of lease grant rights of pasture in 'the common pasture called Kail now recently enclosed' (Thorpe), 'within the enclosed pasture now known by the name of New Pasture,' etcetera. At the same time, cottagers and householders in the villages were allowed to enclose small 'crofts' of ground immediately surrounding their houses, for the growing of special crops, hemp for linen, and grain for their own use or that of their animals. Under Queen Elizabeth it had been made legal for communities to enclose part of the waste and of the common fields, to encourage a better tilth of the most exhausted arable land. Six or seven centuries of continuous cropping, with an inadequate rotation of crops and little in the way of careful manuring, had led to the exhaustion of the ground. The enclosure in small fields allowed each individual to get the use of the manure of his own stock, and to practise some improvements in his methods of agriculture. The Elizabethan enclosures were common in the south and midlands, but had little effect in the north beyond encouraging the enclosure of more numerous crofts near the houses. In all our villages, however, the crofts were abundant, and the leases of houses and farms show that an

Back Lane, Grassington, showing in the background the straight lines of enclosure walling.

average house had with it four or five closes or crofts, sometimes making allowance of wood and underwood from the waste for the repair of fences, but often allowing the right of getting stone from the waste to make and maintain walls round the enclosures. Much of the stone so got was not quarried but cleared from the land.

These closes make the irregular, crazy patterns near the villages — each tenant walling in a portion, usually from half to one acre, occasionally a little more, making his wall where it was convenient, winding a little to include large boulders and blocks of stone, or going at a curve to meet some other wall or fence. In these older walls, it is common to find their base including monstrous single blocks and boulders, often a ton or more in weight, two or three feet high and as much long, standing on edge like rows of giant teeth. The wall includes and is built on to them. Partly from first design and largely by age such walls are curly and bulging, hardly a straight line to be found among them.

During the whole of the 16th and early 17th century, as the common field system broke down and independent farmers began to flourish, strips and holdings in common fields were exchanged, small portions of land and rights were consolidated, and by agreement and exchange small fields were enclosed on the borders of the old common fields and on all open spaces around the village. Again in these, the walling followed very little plan beyond the convenience of the enclosure and the available material. These walls are squat and irregular, of great thickness in stony ground, aimed partly at clearing the soil of stones, and added to from time to time. There is little coursing of the stones in the wall, nor any regularity of size; anything that came to hand was incorporated in the fence.

During the latter part of the 18th century there was an increasing powerful demand throughout the country for sub-division and enclosure of the common fields and moors. This demand came not from the mass of the people but from the few who were experimenting in new ways of agriculture, the landed gentry who wanted more land on which to increase their flocks and herds, and the politically-minded who saw a menace in the independence of the commoner who possessed common rights, who had his own cow and a few sheep, a share in the common field, and needed to work for a wage or under regulation only part of his time. Townshend had introduced the cultivation of the turnip which would enable stock to be fed throughout the winter, instead of all but the brood stock being killed off and salted down for winter meat, and with this had worked out a new and immensely more beneficial rotation of cropping the land. Bakewell had experimented with selective breeds of sheep and Culley had carried this forward with sheep and cattle breeding in the Cheviots. Tull introduced horse hoeing and the horse drill for seed sowing, while others recorded the benefits of controlled manuring and land owners were desirous of trying out the newer agriculture but saw no hopes of applying it to the large common fields and rough pastures of the wastes, and looked to enclosure as the only chance of an agricultural revival. As a result of political and economic pressure, enclosure became a live issue, private Acts of Parliament were promoted, giving powers to enclose, and eventually in 1801 a general consolidating Act was obtained by which the procedure of enclosure was systemised and made profitable to the promoters. It was under these Acts that most of the walling of the Dales was built, and to understand the custom of the walls, their making, repair and maintenance, it will be necessary to explore the general procedure of enclosure.

The earlier enclosures were made by consent or by Act of Parliament. In a township where the influential farmers or landowners felt that the time was ripe for enclosure of the commons, an individual or a group which represented not less than a third of the total interest (this was assured if the Lord of the Manor, the holder of the great tithes, and one or two principal farmers combined) would draw up a scheme for enclosure, petition Parliament for leave to introduce a Bill, which on introduction was referred after a second reading to a committee which could receive petitions against the Bill; the Bill, returned to the House, would be passed, sent to the Lords, and receive Royal assent. The Bill named Commissioners who would then attend on the land, and re-distribute all common holdings and extinguish common rights. Before 1774 it was possible for a single individual to promote an enclosure, and there was no obligation upon him to inform his neighbours that this was being done, but in 1774 it was ordered that all petitions should be affixed to the parish church doors three Sundays in August or September.

The committee to consider the Bill in Parliament was entirely biased. The report of Parliament in 1825 says 'under the present system each Bill is committed to the Member who is charged with its management and such other Members as he may choose to name from the same and adjoining counties and consequently it has been practically found that the Members to whom the Bills have been committed have been generally those who have been the most interested in the result.' Petitions against a Bill were presented in person or by a solicitor, and so the small man was prevented from making any effectual protest. The Commissioners appointed were usually three in number, lawyers or agents, who promoted a survey of all the common lands included in the Bill, then proceeded to extinguish common rights, and to re-allot all land among the promoters plus the common field and common right holders. The promoters took the lion's share. When allotment of lands had been made, the various householders found themselves with small fields or enclosures allotted to them from the old common fields or from the waste, with the duty incumbent upon them of fencing these within a certain period. The cost of the promotion of the Bill, the fees of Commissioners' surveyors, etcetera, where charges upon the land, and the Commissioners had power to sell sufficient land to recover expenses, the promoters usually buying cheap and so enlarging their estate. The cost of walling the enclosure and a share of the cost of promotion was to be paid by all who received an allotment, and if they failed to pay, as was often the case with some of the smaller holders, their land could be sold or leased at rent by the Commissioners to recover costs. The enclosures were a tragedy for the small man; he lost his right of pasturage on the common, lost his bit of land, and was compelled to become a wage labourer in a time of falling wages and rising cost of living. It secured the enslavement of the labouring classes.

Now let us come to the walling. A few actual quotations from enclosure Acts will illustrate the various points. In 1788 'an Act for Dividing and Inclosing the several stinted Pastures . . . in the township of Grassington . . .' was obtained. The preamble to the Act says 'And whereas by reason of the Largeness of the said four stinted Pastures, Trespasses are frequently committed therein, by Persons turning cattle thereon, who have no right to any of the Cattle Gates on the said Pastures to the great damage and prejudice of the owners . . .' it was proposed that the pastures be divided and enclosed. Henry Waddington of Crow Nest, Thomas Chippendale of Skipton and Thomas Ingleby of Austwick, gentlemen, were appointed Commissioners. Among other provisions, the Commissioners 'shall order all persons within the space of Twelve Months to inclose, ditch, fence, wall, etc., such parts as shall be directed.' They are to have stones for walling from such parts as shall be set out for that purpose, etcetera. Roads are set out and the owners of adjoining enclosures are ordered to wall them. In the award of the Commissioners we get the following clauses: 'Then as to the manner in which all and every of the said several Allotments or Shares of the said several proprietors and interested Persons in, and upon the several Pastures, shall be divided one from another. WE DO hereby Order and Award that the same shall be done by good stone Walls, in all places made 34 Inches broad in the Bottom and 6 Feet high, under a Stone not exceeding 4 Inches in

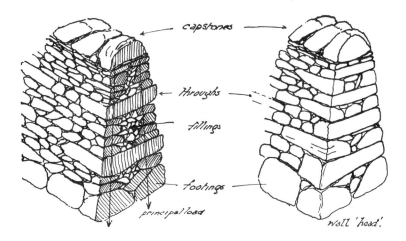

thickness, which shall be laid upon, and cover the Tops of the Walls in every Part, that there shall be laid in a Workman-like Manner 21 good Throughs in every Rood of Fence, and the first 12 to be laid on at a height of 2 Feet broad, and the second 9 to be laid on at the height of 4 Feet from the Ground, and the Wall Batter to decrease gradually from the Bottom to the Tops which shall not be less anywhere than 16 Inches broad under the uppermost Stone . . .' '. . . Now Therefor we do hereby Certify that we have calculated and proportioned the Length and Expenses of all such new Fences according to the best of our Judgements and deliberately and impartially considered how much and what parts of the same, the several Owners and Proprietors ought in Reason and Equity to erect and make . . .'

The award then proceeds to catalogue, owner by owner, the walling to be made, in a cumbrous verbal form repeated word by word in every case. The general form is as follows: 'We Order and Award that the said Stephen Hartley, or the future Owner or Owners of his several Allotments or Shares upon the several Pastures for the time being shall for, and in respect thereof, erect and make or cause and procure to be erected and made at his and their own proper Expence all the fences on the West side of his said Allotment No. 1 upon the said Pasture called the Old Pasture . . . also all the Fence on the East side of his said Allotment No. 43 . . . and such part of the Out Fence dividing his Allotment No. 64 from the said Common or Moor called Grassington Moor . . .' and so on through all his allotments and strips adjoining the roads. It follows that in general, each person walls two sides of his fields, occasionally three if one side adjoins a road. The portion walled by each person is set out on the map which accompanies the award, and is marked by a small T mark placed with its foot on the wall line and its head into the field whose owner builds the wall. On the ground, each length of wall built by one person is carried to a 'wall-head,' a clean finished division line, and the position and condition of the wall-heads is a matter of great importance when walls come to be repaired. Looking at a field with several gaps in the walls, awaiting repair, a farmer will tell you, pointing to different parts of the field: 'Them gaps belong to Jimmie, these here are mine, there's a wall-head over yonder between us.'

The enclosure Act and award for the common fields of Linton was obtained in 1792 and makes similar provision for walling all enclosures with walls 6 feet high, 3 feet broad at the base and battered to 14 inches wide at the top with 21 through stones per rood. This enclosure award is of great interest as both the map and the description show a large area of 'ancient enclosures' immediately around the village, with the common fields a little further away, and the common pastures out on Linton Moor. The common fields were divided up by the award into small straight-walled and rectangular fields generally about eight acres or so in area, and the old common pasture and moor was cut into long strips up to thirty or more acres. In the award map and on the ground there is a clear portrayal of the three types of walling, the drunken irregular maze of the older enclosures, the geometrical mesh of the common fields, and the mile-long ruled walls of the out pasture.

Changes in the enclosure procedure in 1844 led to a few further enclosures to the moors up and down the Dales country, but the main part of the enclosures were made and walled between 1780 and 1820, so that most of the straight walls are at least 150 and possibly 190 or more years old, the crooked small croft walling nearer the village being possibly 200 to 300 years old.

2.   Building the Walls

BEFORE proceeding to describe the actual craft of walling as practised under the enclosure awards, it is interesting to note that there are a few places in the Dales which were walled without the intermediary of an Act and award, and in many cases in the century or more preceding the enclosure movement. Gunnerside is perhaps the most complete example of an open-field area, gradually enclosed by 'intake,' small fields added one to the other by mutual agreement and exchange, during a long and indefinite period. Here the maze of walls behind the village is made up entirely of curly, crooked portions, enclosing small irregular fields. A close examination of the walls shows that each is roughly in the nature of an extension into the old open field using the walls of the last previous field as much as possible. The walls themselves have utilised all the large stones that were cleared off the land, and wander about seeking both easy ground and convenience in building. The lanes from the village to the common pastures and moors, and to the various fields, are just wide fragments of green left between walls that are related not to the roads but to the fields, and so they vary constantly in width and direction, and still provide a large area of common pasture.

There are comparable areas near many villages — the upper green at Hebden is a remnant of the old common left unwalled, while the whole slope from the beck, on the east side up to Scar Top and Edge Top is enclosed with ancient walling of most irregular pattern. One of the earliest examples of this early walling is preserved above Malham Tarn, around Middle House. Here in the midst of 18th century straight ruled enclosure walls is a small oasis of curly walled enclosures, some of them going back to the late monastic days of the 16th century and possibly earlier, when the monks of Fountains Abbey had a sheep farm here, the nucleus of the area is the old sheep folds near the site of the original house, with small crofts and fields added to them from time to time. Similar patches of early enclosures are to be found in most parts of the Dales; there are a few in Bowland, a few in the Calder valley, and many in the northern Dales.

In these ancient enclosures the walls tend to be variants of one main pattern. Large stones and boulders, often two or three feet in their main dimension, have been rolled off the ground that was being cleared, and arranged in a rough double wall around the sides. In many cases a small natural outcrop, or a sharp natural feature has been utilised as a foundation. The large boulders define the wall foot, and this is often two or even three yards wide; indeed I have measured the base of some of these old walls as much as twelve feet wide in an extreme example. Stones of all kinds and shapes cleared from the ground are then piled between the double row of large footings, to form the base of a pyramidal heap. Partly from original structure and partly by centuries of settlement, these walls now approximate to a blunt pyramid on an average six to nine feet broad at the base, and only about four feet high. They are literally piled up, with little building about them. Their stability is that of a well piled heap of stones.

If we turn to the enclosure walling, there is evidently a very definite method and craft of building, with a fair uniformity of method over a wide area. The reports on the state of agriculture, made for the Board of Agriculture between 1790 and 1810, all include a section on fences, and in those for the northern counties we get some information both of the size and cost of dry walls. Broun, reporting on the West Riding in 1799, says: 'As to the manner of inclosing, we know no fence equal to a good quickset hedge of white thorn. Perhaps stone walls are more elegible where sheep are kept. These we would recommend to be built, or rather lipped with lime, and to be six quarters in height (i.e. six quarter yards, or 4 feet 6 inches) with an additional quarter by way of capping. Probably this at the long run is the cheapest fence, but, being very expensive at first, it should in every case be executed by the proprietor, the tenant paying legal interest upon the outlays.' Bailey says for County Durham, 1810: 'In some parts of the country where the land is too high to grow hedges, or the climate too bad, stone walls are used as fences. The usual dimensions are — width at bottom 2 feet 4 inches; top 1 foot 4 inches; height 4½ feet; and a coping of 9 inches making the height in all 5 feet 3 inches. The expense of getting and walling the stone is 7s. per rood of seven yards; the expense of leading depends upon the distance; and on an average may be taken as the same as the winning and walling, making the whole expense about 14s. per rood.'

Farey made a voluminous report on Derbyshire between 1800 and 1813, and speaks at length about the walling. His first argument is one that has been too seldom expressed, and one which no recent writer on agriculture has noticed. He says that the average fields are only four or five acres in extent; 'supposing each five acre field fenced on three sides in order to allow for Fences against Roads and irregular fields, and allowing twelve links or eight feet wide for a hedge and ditch, the quantity of land so occupied is 39 Perches or one twentieth part of the Field; and if the Fences are Walls, as is general in the districts alluded to, occupying or spoiling not more than four links wide, the quantity of land thus lost is but one sixtieth of the whole.' He does not point out a further argument, that a hedge, besides taking up a much greater width, takes nourishment from the adjacent soil, needs many years to reach suitable proportions, and needs frequent cutting, laying and replacing of plants. A wall soundly built is good for a hundred years, and the labour and cost spent on the same length of wall and hedge, counting the occasional gap repairs to the wall and the regular trimming of the hedge, etcetera, with the original cost, is only a fraction in the case of the stone wall to that of the hedge. Farey says: 'A wall fence is no sooner finished than the full benefit of it is reaped, either for the protection of Crops or Shelter;

14

whereas in planting Hedges, Wood must be procured to protect the young fences and constant care and expense in weeding, etc., must be incurred for several years before any benefit is derived from the Hedge. Wall fences in the Peak Hundreds, are usually built dry without any mortar, five feet high, with a nine inch coping of stones on edge on them, for Boundaries; and four feet and a half, and a nine inch coping for internal Fences; the cost from 6s. to 10s. and 12s. per rood, of seven yards in length, for getting the stone, carting, and building the wall.'

The earliest note we have of the cost of drystone walling is that given by Arthur Young in his *Six Months Tour in the North of England* describing Scroope's work at Dalton near Richmond: 'His first business was the inclosure which he did by walling; the surface of the moor yielded in some places a sufficiency of stones but in many other pits were sunk for them . . . the quarries are all limestone. The first year (1755) 280 roods were built of the ring fence. This work was all contracted for by measures at 5s. 6d. a rood of seven yards long, and 5 feet high. A gate, two posts, and the irons came to 6s.' Bray in his *Tour Through Yorkshire and parts of Derbyshire* in 1777, in passing from Kilnsey to Malham, describes the green road we all know so well. 'This ride is truly wild and romantic; nature here sits in solitary grandeur on the hills, which are lofty, green to the top, and rise in irregular heaps on all hands, in their primaeval state of pasture, without the least appearance of a plough, or habitation for many miles. In the summer they afford good keep for cattle, great numbers of which are taken in to feed from April or May to Michaelmas . . . The pasturage for a Horse for that time is 14s.; a cow 7s.; a sheep 1s.6d. Many of these pastures, which are of great extent, have been lately divided by stone walls of about two yards high, one yard wide at the bottom, lessening to a foot at the top. A man can make about seven yards in length of this in a day, and is paid from 20d. to 2s. The stones brought and laid down for him cost about 7s. more.'

From a great number of enclosure awards, and by measurement in many parts of the North of England, it becomes clear that the walls vary roughly between the following limiting dimensions; height ranges from 5 feet 3 inches to 6 feet, width at the base from 3 feet to 2 feet 4 inches, and at the top from 1 foot 4 inches to 1 foot. In nearly all places the throughs are 21 to the rood, but vary between two rows and three rows. The walls are always capped with a row of coping stones, except in occasional parts of Weardale, where a row of sods is built in at the top, and the matted roots bond the top stones together. The variation in width and height is largely related to the material available for the wall. Where the bulk of the stone is land clearings and rounded boulders, the wall base is made wide and the wall given a good batter, but in the districts of lower Airedale and south of that, where the thin bedded Coal Measure and Millstone Grit flagstones are abundant, the walls are thinner and steeper faced. In an important wall, the coping, called indifferently 'capstones,' 'tops' or 'copings,' is sometimes set in a lime-sand mortar, and this binds the top together, and to a large extent preserves the

15

Walling a gap. *This page — top:* Typical gap; *bottom:* A large gap repaired and ready for the top stones which are laid out in a long line. *Opposite page:* A completed wall, with large through stones and shaped top.

wall from 'gapping' of the type started by sheep jumping and knocking off the capstones.

Let us now follow the process of building a drystone wall. First, when the line has been sèt out, the ground is cleared, sod and soil taken off in a trench about four feet wide, and taken down on to the firm subsoil. In this the foundation 'footing' is made by setting two rows of large squarish boulders with their squared ends facing on the two edges of the wall bottom, and their rougher ends facing inward. In all the walling, an effort is made to get a good 'bed' on to each stone, on which it will sit firmly, and a rough 'end' at right angles to the bed. The end makes the outer face of the wall, and the other sides of the stone don't much matter, almost any shape can be fitted in by a good waller. The 'end' and 'bed' are often just roughly scappelled with a three or four pound hammer, for the foundation and lower courses of the wall. The spaces between the two rows of footings are then filled in with large irregular fillings of any shape, put in so that as few spaces as possible are left. For 'fillings' in all parts of the wall, angular irregular fragments are best, as they are needed to 'bite' and bind together under pressure. This foundation layer should be as solid and firm as can be got, as on its stability depends the life of the wall. Old wallers of sixty years ago used to speak of 'setting a wall on its feet,' and of 'giving it summat to stand on' — in the great majority of large gaps in the walls, when the bottom is 'rid out,' that is, all the fallen stuff cleared, the trouble is seen to be footings that have shifted or tilted, or occasionally footing stones that 'have a Charlie,' that is, are round-backed and have not been well filled. The second layer or 'course' is laid on them, each stone resting on two below, built over the joint of the bottom course. The stones in each course are laid so that they are 'level through' the wall, wedged firmly in that position with small stones and packed up behind with 'fillings.' It is a great temptation in making a wall to let the course lie a little bit into the wall, to let the stones tilt a little bit backwards, but it is essential, as will be seen later, that every course lies with its stones horizontal, and the batter of the wall is got by setting each course back just a little behind the one below. The wall is built in two faces, the best stones being picked from the heap, and laid to make a continuous course as near the same height as possible right along the run of the wall. The spaces between their inside ends, and the middle of the wall is filled with 'fillings.' Now the rough broken stone used as filling is not thrown in, but a first-class waller will put it in, dropping or placing each bit carefully, so as to leave no space unfilled, and so that the fillings grip and tighten on one another as the wall grows.

An old waller in one of the northern Dales, teaching his son to wall over sixty years ago, used to say that fillings thrown in would 'side' the walling stones out of position. He claimed that a man who shovelled his fillings in was no waller. His son remembers that 'after the day's work was done and the length of wall coped, he would stand back a yard or two and then run up and force his foot right on to the wall between the bottom and top through; if there was no "rattle" of shifting fillers and no pushing out of the wallers, he would say it was well filled and sound.' A common method is for two men to wall face to face, one on each side, with possibly a boy to place fillings. The fillings must keep pace with the rising faces, and must back up and fix all the wedging stones needed to level the courses. As the wall grows, the stones used become smaller and smaller, and successive courses shallower. One old waller said he always walled with only the best stone, because each time he stooped to take one off the loose heap, he picked out the largest and best, and continued to do so all day; in following this plan of course the waller sets on one side all the stones he will want for coping — it is a sad experience at the end of the day to see one's capstones built into the bottom of a five foot wall, and the top unfinished.

The throughs are long stones which go across from side to side, sometimes just the width of the wall at the part where they are built in, sometimes longer and sticking out like steps of a stile. The throughs are necessary to bind the two faces together and prevent the wall 'bellying out' and bursting. A 'weel thruffed wall' rarely fails unless the foundations slip, and even then the gap is never very serious. Throughs have generally to be carted for a wall, sandstone flags being the best if they are chosen two or three inches thick. The two sides of the wall are brought carefully to the same level, and a good bed made each side before the through is laid on. The first lot is generally put on at about two feet from the footings, and another lot about four feet up, but in some walls there is a third set of thinner throughs just under the copings. It is often asked why throughs are left with ragged ends sticking out of a wall or a building — it is laborious to cut a through exactly to the right length before building it in, and when it is built in it is unwise to break off the ends by hammering because the through can be damaged in the thickness of the wall and the damage not be seen. Better a ragged end than a cracked through. When the wall is high enough for the coping, the top is filled off and levelled with thin slabby stones or even small flags in some places, and the coping stones placed on these. The tops are generally roughly semi-circular with their straight side, the diameter, the same as the width of the wall top. This rests right across, bridging the wall top and binding the two faces together. The capstones are thinner than they are high and usually lean one against the other, all in the same direction.

The capping of the wall offers play to many fashions and fancies of the individual builders, and probably varies more than any other feature of the walls. In walls that have a high finish the capstones are cut to size with a hammer and the whole topping is made to range in a continuous and smooth line. The semi-circular top is the most popular for this work, the stones being rough dressed to the shape of half a cheese and placed with the straight side down. In these fine dressed stones there is usually no appreciable leaning. The commonest topping is made of irregular stones which are brought only very roughly to a size, and these are set on edge leaning heavily one way. At a convenient wall-head a really massive bolster stone is set, then the caps lean against this and one another. The reason for this is very sound. All drystone walls 'give' and settle from time to time, and as they do so the caps can adjust themselves, still leaning on one another and so held in place. It is not easy to lift or knock out a single cap from such a wall. As the weight of the caps is necessary to hold the wall together, this 'flexibility' of the topping is very important. In some cases the tops are set in mortar, but usually this

leads, sooner or later, to deterioration of the wall. If there is any settlement, the capping forms a rigid bar which cannot 'follow' the wall but remains suspended in space as a bridge across the settled part. Relieved of the top weight, this part soon breaks out and 'gaps.'

In some areas a neat top is made by 'buck and doe,' that is by alternating high and low top stones or putting an extra high one at regular intervals. Some walls are topped off with a carefully set row of large flags, with big rounded tops set on top of them; on many walls the throughs immediately under the tops are allowed to project some distance on one side, and thus act as a deterrent to jumping sheep.

The completed wall is really a structure in equilibrium, the main pressures, the weight of the tops and wall faces being carried right down each face, through the carefully laid coursed wall stones on to the foundations. Each stone spans on to two below it and each stone is safely wedged and firm. The two faces are held together against any tendency to bulge outward by the throughs. The fillings give solidity, preventing the walls bulging inwards, and if properly placed, they bind and leave no spaces for movement of the wall stones. Where accident, or too keen rabbiters have removed a wall stone and allowed fillings to fall out, leaving a hollow part in the wall, a collapse soon follows. Similarly where capstones are knocked off and not replaced the two sides soon loosen and fall apart.

Wall head, with marks and "cripple hole".

Each length of wall is brought to a 'head' at all openings, and at the termination of walls belonging to different people. The 'head' is built by making a course of the massive throughs straight over the footings at the wall ends, and following by a couple of large stones almost like throughs for size, built on to the through and lying in the face of the wall with their squared end

20

carrying up the square corner. Throughs and large corners continue right to the top, so there is a clean joint or vertical finish to the wall at the head. On steep slopes, where the wall is going up the slope, it is customary to include heads at frequent intervals. If a wall on a steep slope starts to 'gap,' the wall on the up side will fall for a very great length unless heads are built, when the fall usually stops at the next head. In such steep walls, as in all positions, the courses are kept horizontal so that one course starting at the footings will, as you go downhill, rapidly rise to the top of the wall, and the stones on the same course will be large at the ground level and get smaller as the wall top is approached. Where the wall runs along a steep hillside the batter is usually all on the downhill side, and the uphill side is practically vertical.

Many of the larger boundary walls have been built in small sections by the different freeholders, each section being finished with a wall-head. In many cases, each section is marked at the footings at the bottom of each head with the mark of the person responsible for the maintenance of that section. Such marks are initials and geometric marks of all kinds, but most of them are identical with the marks previously mentioned as used to indicate the different 'lots' in common meadow, and in the common fields.

3. Builders of the Walls

WHEN the walls are built gateways are made, and the gates have as much character as the walls. The commonest method of hanging is to have a large gatepost of gritstone at each side of the opening, and on the hinge side to hang the gate with one 'creak,' or hook, near the top of the post, and let the foot of the gate, armed with a wrought iron stirrup and peg, rest on a socket stone set in the ground. The gate is balanced so that it will open easily, but if left before being fully open will swing back to the closed position. Mostly the creak is on the same side of the gatepost as a wall face, and the gate lies when shut against the front of the two gate stoops.

Other openings left in the walls are 'cripple holes' for sheep — low square openings closed by a loose flag large enough to allow sheep to pass from one pasture to another if the flag is removed, but not large enough for cattle. These are called 'smout holes' further north. Stiles are made differently in different districts. The simplest form is to arrange three or four throughs to project as successive steps, with a gap in the copings through which the top step is continuous. Others are made by bringing the wall to two heads 18 inches or so apart, and placing a thin stoop at each side within the gap, one nearly the height of the wall, the other only half the height. These are close enough at the bottom to prevent the passage of sheep, but the short stump at one side leaves room for the thicker end of the foot passenger to pass.

The walling materials show very wide variation, and follow closely the geology of the ground. Carrying was always reduced to a minimum, and most wall stones have not travelled far from where they occurred; on many

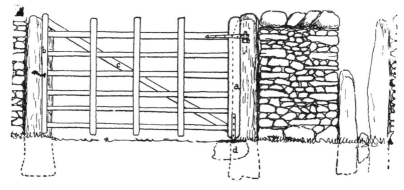

Gate and stile: (a) artree; (b) gatehead; (c) swape; (d) socket stone.

Openings in dry walls. *Top:* Gateway showing evidence of former wider opening. *Bottom:* Stile.

of the fells a wall will be for a distance grey-white, built of clean looking limestone, then for a few yards be dappled like a badger then pass on to dark brown or black. The dark is of grit, and the change coincides within a yard or two with the passage from limestone to grit in the solid rock, or may, as near Stockdale and along the road from Settle to Malham, mark the crossing of the Craven Fault. On the fells in Wensleydale and the upper slopes of the other Dales, the alternations of grits and limestones in the Yoredale series are marked by strips of dark and light wall as the walls climb to the watersheds. In other districts the change from Millstone Grits to coal measures is marked by the change from rough wall stones to fine even coursed flags with thinner straighter walls. The throughs in parts of Wharfedale and much of Ribblesdale are made from large slabs broken from glacial erratics of Silurian slate.

At the time of the enclosure Acts and until the end of the 19th century, a good waller would build a rood (7 yards) of wall a day, having the help of a boy to place fillings. It is still a tradition in the Dales that old wallers working on the fell side would, on arriving at the wall in the morning, throw the heaviest hammer some way up the hillside, and declare that as the length to be walled that day. For new walling a frame is generally used, two battens fastened together at the correct batter of the wall faces, and reared up at the ends of the section to be built; a line is then stretched from frame to frame and the wall built by the line. For short lengths and gap walling most wallers work by 'rake o' th' eye.'

Much has been written of the 'lost art' of dry walling. In the Dales there is still a surprising large body of men, farmers and farm labourers, who are skilled at this job, and who carry forward the traditional craft. The burden of extra work placed on farming these last thirty years or so, has led to a vast increase in slap-dash gap walling, rearing up anything that will discourage sheep from getting through, but where time can be afforded there are still many men who can wall up to the old standards. The walling competitions at Kilnsey Show and at many of the Young Farmers' Club meets will do much to preserve the tradition, and in any programme of agricultural reconstruction there should be a good provision for the encouragement of walling as a craft. It will take many years to repair our walls into sound condition. A few strands of wire and a concrete post or two are no substitute for a good wall in rough weather. In rain, sheep sheltering under the wall keep dry and comfortable; the heaviest of the rains is sheltered off, and the draughts which come through all dry walls keep the fleeces dried out.

The extent of walling in the Pennines represents many life-times of patient skill spent on hard manual work. We benefit today by the work of these generations, and it is incumbent upon us to maintain the walls in good repair. It is to be hoped that the miles of wire fence introduced into the Dales during the war will not find its way into gap stopping, but that good walling will be resumed. There is no day more satisfying than one spent high up on the fell side, in a bright autumn or spring, working steadily at one of these

A team of wallers at work.

old walls. Ridding out a gap gives one great respect for the strength that brought and laid the foundations. The wall represents in sheer physical strength more than appears at first sight. Three feet wide battering to 16 inches and 6 feet high, reckoning the space between fillings and stones at about one third the total volume, a wall takes rather more than 1¾ tons of stone per yard. Seven yards a day means more than 12 tons have been lifted the height of a yard. With the shorter working day the waller now lifts much less than this, but still moves enough cold stone to make the frequent stops to warm the fingers at a wood fire kept burning close at hand a great pleasure. Looking across the dale and seeing the miles of walls in valley bottom and on steep hillside, one realises the real monumental effort they represent, and there is a great thrill to be found in maintaining or adding to the permanent mark on the pattern of the countryside that they make.

As the walls belong to more than one period of building, so the labour that built them is different both in character and organisation for the different groups of walling. Of the earliest enclosures of the 16th and 17th centuries we know little beyond the fact that they were mainly the work of the community, each person with common rights on the waste or moor, or on the common pastures, contributing his appropriate share of the building of the wall. As the individual sections were only short, it was rare for an outside mason to be employed, each person being able at some time or other during

25

the year to build up the portion allotted to him. The extent of this early wall, apart from the closes around the houses, was not very great, the principal pasture, often of several hundred acres, and occasionally the boundary wall between the pasture of two different townships, being most of what was built. The building was levied as a 'payne' upon the holders of common rights, by the Bylawmen, or Bylawgravemen, the jury annually appointed in each township to be responsible for the common pastures. The Bylawmen were elected at a towns-meeting when absentees were fined one shilling. Usually there were four Bylawmen each year. The Bylaws of Giggleswick in 1654 include an item:

'That every Tennant and Inhabitant shall make their partes of the out-Dykes about Gigglesweeke fields a yarde and a half high, for every default 3s. 4d. (fine).'

In 1602 there is a further law added, relating to the walls of closes adjoining the roads:

'Item if any person or persons suffer his wall stones to fall into the high way and the stones to be there to the annoyance of passengers travelling that way shall forfeit 3s. 4d.'

The Bylawmen had the care of all 'town' property, the maintenance of fences (walls), the regulation of common pasture, etcetera. An example from Bordley, at the time that it was a flourishing village in the 17th century, but since depopulated, will illustrate again the procedure with regard to the

maintenance of walls around the common pastures. February 8th, 1647: 'Bylaws and orders made and agreed upon by Cuthbert Wade, William Tenant, Thomas Tenant and Simon Wilkinsonne, Bylawmen elected and chosen for this present year for the good ordering and governing of their goods, pastures and fences, and for good neighbourhood to be done and kept amongst we whose names are subscribed hereafter agreed upon and made by the said Bylawmen and condescended to by the reaste of the Inhabitants as followeth — Imprimis wee do order and sett downe that every inhabitant or owner of any grounde in the severell pastures within the lordship of Bordley aforesaid or any of them shall make and repair his geates and fences belonging the same before the first day of April next and that everyone that shall offend in breaking this Bylaw shall forfeit 3s. 4d.'

In 1680 the Bylawmen of Settle agreed upon a payne for the walls of the common pastures. October 6th, 1680: 'Then a payne laid by the ffreeholders and tennants of Settle and such of them as have right upon that pasture called Scalber belonging Settle aforesaid that the ffreeholders and tenants of Long Preston or such of them as of right ought to repayre the walls and fences betwixt the moores and pastures belonging the Township of Long Preston and Settle aforesaid that they the said ffreeholders and tenants of Long Preston doe repayre their fences betwixt the said townships, and especially all theyr fences betwixt the said Scaleber and the Horseclose and Ragdbirke and betwixt Goodmans mosse belonging to Settle and the said Ragdbirke betwixt now and the fifteenth day of April now next coming Sufficient to turn beaste and cowe upon paine of every roode of fence in defaulte five shillings the one moiety to the lord of the Manor and the other moiety of the ffreeholders and tenants of Settle.'

Many similar pains were made by the Bylawmen of many of the villages, laying upon the freeholders the duty first of building the common pasture and boundary walls, and afterwards of maintaining them in repair. After the enclosures, the common pastures that had been closed were put in charge of a paid shepherd who was appointed yearly, and in many cases the maintenance of the pasture walls was made a part of his duties.

The building of the enclosure walls presented a problem of a different kind. In the earlier cases, where enclosure had been made by common consent, the enclosers could agree amongst themselves how soon and by what method the walling was to be accomplished. Some examples of this method of enclosure are found in the Dales, mainly before 1790. At Settle, all the gate-holders of Settle who had sheep or cattle gates on Settle Bank, High Scar and Scaleber Pasture, some of the pastures administered by the Bylawmen, as just quoted, were called to a public meeting on January 26th, 1757. It was there proposed that these pastures should be enclosed by common consent. The meeting agreed to abide by the decisions of five Commissioners who should be independent gentlemen, known to them, and for this purpose selected Thomas Carr of Stackhouse, Richard Clapham of Feizor, Stephen Knowles of Newby, Henry Waddington of Crow Nest, and

William Bradley of Giggleswick. A private Bill was obtained in Parliament, allowing this enclosure, and the Commissioners proceeded to allot the lands, and to make conditions for the walling and all other allowances, according to the desires of the gate-holders who promoted the award. The allotment holders would then wall their own portions, or at their discretion employ a waller.

In the case where a landowner or one or two private individuals had promoted an enclosure Act and award under the procedure that was common after 1780, the case was very different. When an award had been made, the Commissioners in all cases set a short term limit during which the walls had to be built to a definite plan and size appointed by them. The amount of walling ran into many miles, and was far beyond the capacity of the freeholders sharing in the award to complete. For these walls outside masons were employed, or free men from the land who took up walling as a profession. The enclosure Commissioners reserved the right, if any allotment was not walled, to hire wallers to complete the fences and to sell or let the allotment for a term, until the rent received had paid for the cost of the walls. In many awards the Commissioners hired gangs of wallers to complete most of the walls, and apportioned the total cost among all persons sharing the award in the proportion of their allotment. This was by far the most satisfactory way, and its effect is seen in some townships in the perfect uniformity of the walling over the whole area enclosed. This would never have been achieved if each man walled his own piece when and how he could; the variations in skill would have been obvious.

There are not many sources from which we can learn much about the walling squads, but sufficient has been preserved to allow us to construct some picture of their status and habits. Hugh Miller, the Scottish geologist, in his youth was apprenticed as a mason, and about 1820 — other work being scarce — he and his master joined with other masons to make a squad, which was employed intermittently in quarrying stone, doing small agricultural buildings and walling. He describes the life of the mason squads as very rough; they moved in spring to the area to be walled, or where the building was to be done, and set up for themselves in an old barn or building that the landowner allowed them to use. Here they made bunks for sleeping, had small fires for cooking their meals, largely of oatmeal cakes and porridge and here they lived as a company during all the summer and autumn, returning in winter when the frost prevented their work, to their own crofts and smallholdings.

Of the character of his workmates in general, he says: 'He is in general a blunt, manly, taciturn fellow . . . His employment is less purely mechanical than many others, he is not like a man ceaselessly engaged in pointing needles or fashioning pin-heads. On the contrary every stone he lays or hews demands the exercise of a certain amount of judgement for itself; and so he cannot wholly suffer his mind to fall asleep over his work. Accustomed to ascertain the straightness of a line at a glance, and to cast his eye along plane walls in order to determine the rectitude of the masonry, he acquires a sort of mathematical precision in determining the true bearings and positions of objects. The mason is always a silent man; the strain on his respiration is too great, when he is actively employed, to leave the necessary freedom to the organ of speech. Living in small villages or cottages in the country they can very rarely procure employment in the neighbourhood of their dwellings, and so they are usually content to regard these as simply their homes for the winter and early spring months when they have nothing to do.'

In Wensleydale, about the beginning of the 19th century, many men left the mines at a period of depression and found occupation in enclosure walling. Two brothers of my great grandmother were employed about 1800 in the lead mines at Keld Heads, near Leyburn. One was a 'level man,' walling the sides and arches of levels in soft ground, the other a shaft hand, walling and repairing shafts, etcetera. With a reduction of output from the mines, they removed into Cotterdale to work for a time on a small coal mine being opened there, but soon found better occupation in offering themselves as masons for the walling of the newly enclosed commons in Mallerstang. For many years they found a good living in the upper Dales, taking walling by contract for the rood, and undertaking the walling of one person's whole allotments. In the worst parts of winter they worked for some weeks or months in the various small mines or collieries in Garsdale and Cotterdale, or over in Swaledale. Several of their friends and relations adopted the same occupation, walling on a long contract, then returning to their home, in some cases to a small farmstead. Some of the men, of whom there are still records and memories, combined a small farm with walling in the slacker part of the farming year. The father of the men who walled in Mallerstang was a farmer who found a profitable spare time job in opening a quarry and limekiln on Askrigg Moor, and with the help of his two sons, building the Askrigg to Gunnerside road on contract and walling it on each side of the moor.

In Wharfedale, several miners adopted walling as a second occupation. This was particularly suitable as most of the mines were leased on a tributing system, where the miner leased a portion of a vein, under conditions to work in it for a minimum time each month, selling the ore so got to the Lord of the Manor, or smelting his ore at the lord's smelt mill and paying his tribute or royalty on the smelted lead. It was easy with this arrangement to work in the mine in bad weather, and in fine weather to go out walling. The skill in stone cutting in fine walling of shafts and areas of bad ground in the mine, and the familiarity with many kinds of stone, made first-class wallers of many of the miners.

In the second quarter of the 19th century the mining prospects improved, and miners went back to their real work, leaving in the fields only a few masons, who were sufficient for the needs of the later enclosure. The bulk of the enclosure walling was completed by 1820, and later there were only a few Acts for the enclosure of outlying moors and commons, where one or two men were sufficient to cope with all the walling needed. From these are descended men who still keep up the skill of walling, but none of whom were able to make it a full time occupation after the completion of the last enclosures, about 1850. The best of them probably became estate masons, many of them returned to farming and taught their sons to repair and gap the walls in the best tradition.

There is a story often repeated in the Dales in many variants and with many disguises, that the walls were built by gangs of convicts or, alternatively, by prisoners from the French wars or by soldiers disbanded after the French wars. There is no documentary support for this view in this part of the country. Parts of Dartmoor were walled by French prisoners and by convicts, and it may be that Cornish and Devonshire miners, many of whom came to work in the mines of Yorkshire about a hundred years or more ago, brought with them the story of that walling, which, with the passing of time has been partly forgotten and partly transferred to this area.

For Further Study

IT is not possible to give a bibliography on the subject of stone-walling, as little has been written specifically on that subject. The following notes, however, may help a reader wishing to carry the subject a little further in his own district. The enclosure awards by parishes are in many cases filed at the County Council Offices or Records Department, and these will in nearly all cases specify the nature and method of making and keeping fences.

The surveys of the Board of Agriculture at the beginning of the 19th century always include a chapter (chap. vi) on enclosures and fencing, and comments on making stone walls are to be found in some of these. The volumes are always under a title 'A General View of the Agriculture of the County of . . .' and the ones for the northern counties are as follows:

Northumberland	J. Bailey & G. Culley	1805
Durham	J. Bailey	1810
Cumberland	J. Bailey & G. Culley	1805
Westmorland	A. Pringle	1805
Lancashire	J. Holt	1795
Yorkshire W.R.	Rennie, Broun & Shirreff	1794
Yorkshire N.R.	Tuke	1794
Yorkshire E.R.	I. Leatham	1794
Derbyshire	J. Farey	1811

The Derbyshire survey, in vol. II, p.83, has a good discussion of walls and fences.

The best approach to the subject is to make a close examination of the walls in one's own neighbourhood, particularly of enclosures which can be dated. It will soon become evident that there are two or three recognisable styles and varieties in walling and it is not difficult to learn to recognise the work of different·periods.

In addition to the method of building the walls themselves, a great deal can be learned from the pattern the walls follow, and this can be looked for on maps of 2½ inches to the mile scale. You will soon learn to associate definite field patterns with certain periods of enclosure, and will detect unusual patches of pattern which will provide a stimulating subject for research. With close attention to recent work, you may learn to recognise the particular work of some individuals, for most wallers acquire some little trick of their own which gives character to their work.

Finally, carry a sketch book and don't be afraid of trying to draw different bits of wall, taking trouble to note carefully the shape and size of stones and how they are placed one on another. It will not be long before you become quick to recognise the work of different periods and the skill of various now long-forgotten craftsmen.

A.R.